THE GREAT WALL OF CHINA

Essential Events

THE GREAT WALL OF
CHINA

BY JOSEPH O'NEILL

Content Consultant
Ronald G. Dimberg, PhD
Corcoran Department of History, University of Virginia

ABDO
Publishing Company

CREDITS

Published by ABDO Publishing Company, 8000 West 78th Street, Edina, Minnesota 55439. Copyright © 2009 by Abdo Consulting Group, Inc. International copyrights reserved in all countries. No part of this book may be reproduced in any form without written permission from the publisher. The Essential Library™ is a trademark and logo of ABDO Publishing Company.

Printed in the United States.

Editor: Rebecca Rowell
Copy Editor: Paula Lewis
Interior Design and Production: Rebecca Daum
Cover Design: Rebecca Daum

Library of Congress Cataloging-in-Publication Data
O'Neill, Joseph R.
  The Great Wall of China / by Joseph R. O'Neill.
      p. cm. — (Essential events)
  Includes bibliographical references and index.
  ISBN 978-1-60453-513-6
  1. Great Wall of China (China)—History—Juvenile literature. I.
Title.

  DS793.G67O54 2009
  951—dc22

                                    2008033106

TABLE OF CONTENTS

*The Badaling Great Wall near Beijing, China,
is the most visited section of the Great Wall.*

LAND OF ACHIEVEMENTS

China is the largest country in Asia and the world's most populous nation. It also has one of the world's oldest continuous civilizations. The Chinese have occupied their vast territory for thousands of years. The ancient people who lived in the area we know as China were hunters and gatherers. Over time, many of them became farmers who settled and worked the land. These farmers established their homes and farms primarily along three rivers: the *Huang He* (Yellow River), the *Yangzi Jiang* (Yangtze River), and the *Xi Jiang* (West River).

The ancient Chinese referred to their country as *Zhongguo*, the "Middle Kingdom," because they believed they were at the center of the universe. Eventually, settlements joined, and villages became part of the landscape—villages that used walls for defense against neighboring villages and invaders from the north. Villages later merged to become territories that were united into a single empire in 221 BCE.

China boasts numerous achievements in a variety of areas. The country has had many great thinkers and philosophers, including

The Yellow River

The Yellow River is indeed yellow. The river's yellow tint is the result of loess, a very loose and very fine soil comprised of silt and finely ground rock that is deposited in the water by the wind and dissolved. The Chinese also refer to the Yellow River as the "Muddy Flow" because of the large amount of soil dissolved in it.

Painted in the early nineteenth century, this artwork from the Qing dynasty depicts scenes from the life of Confucius and his disciples.

Confucius. Chinese artists have created beautiful works of art, including sculptures, paintings, and calligraphy. Chinese inventors have introduced creations that have changed lives, including the compass, gunpowder, paper and printing, porcelain, silk, and tea. Of the many contributions the Chinese people have made to the world, the Great Wall of China is among the most remarkable and best-known achievements.

World Wonder

The Great Wall, *Chang Cheng* in Chinese, is massive. For thousands of miles, it winds like a snake through China's varied terrain—up and down mountains and through desert, plains, and valleys. In addition, there are smaller walls that extend from the main wall, similar to branches of a tree. Conservative estimates of the Great Wall's length make it 2,400 miles (3,862 km), while other estimates are as much as 3,930 miles (6,325 km). The Great Wall's thickness ranges from 15 to 30 feet (5 to 9 m), and it reaches as high as 25 feet (8 m).

For many centuries, the Great Wall has been considered one of the world's wonders. It is often mistakenly thought of as a single wall. Rather, the Great Wall is a series of walls that were constructed, reconstructed, and expanded over several centuries and, depending

Printing

The Chinese developed a method for printing in the year 590 CE. Initially, the Chinese carved a board with the text for an entire page. Later, they carved individual blocks for words and created movable type circa 1040. This development was well before Guttenberg created his famous printing press in 1450.

= Great Wall

Mongolia

Tongliao

Chifeng

Jinzhou

Zhangjiakou   Chengde   Jinxi

China   Baotou

Huang He (Yellow River)   Beijing ★

Yumen   Tangshan

Wuhai

Jinchuan   Tianjin

Wuhai   Taiyuan   Shijiazhuang

Xining   Jinan

Tianshuibu   Handan

Xiping

Lanzhou   Tai'an

Tongchuan   Xuzhou

Zhengzhou

Xi'an

Guozhen   Zhumadian

Nanjing

Ankang

Xiangfan   Hefei

Wuhan

Chengdu

Zigong   Chongqing   Nanchang

The Great Wall today

on the location, using different materials. Villages
and regions built the initial walls as a means of
defense. Over the centuries, these walls developed
into what we think of as the Great Wall when they
were incorporated into *Wan-Li Chang Cheng*, which
is Chinese for "Long Wall of 10,000 li." A *li* is

a Chinese unit of measure, and 10,000 li is equivalent to 3,107 miles (5,000 km).

The massive construction project was the idea of China's first emperor, Shi Huangdi. He ended more than 250 years of regional fighting between several independent states and united China in 221 BCE. Once in control of a great empire, Shi Huangdi wanted to maintain his power and position. He came up with the idea to create a giant wall along China's northern border to keep out raiders from territories north of China: the Wall of Qin. A wall would also help define his empire and mark a boundary between the Chinese and the people who were not Chinese. Shi Huangdi wanted to keep the Chinese people together and separate from other groups. A wall would isolate the Chinese from foreigners—at least those to the north.

Seven Wonders of the Medieval World

There are several lists of seven world wonders, including those of ancient times, medieval times, modern times, and those that are natural. The Great Wall of China was named a world wonder in a list for the Middle Ages (500–1500 CE). The Seven Wonders of the Medieval World are Stonehenge (England), the Colosseum (Italy), the Catacombs of Kom el Shoqafa (Egypt), the Great Wall (China), the Porcelain Tower of Nanjing (China), the Hagia Sophia (Turkey), and the Leaning Tower of Pisa (Italy).

Construction of the Great Wall continued long after the reign of Shi Huangdi, particularly during the Han dynasty (206 BCE–220 CE) and the Ming dynasty (1368–1644 CE). Han and Ming emperors rebuilt and expanded the Wall of Qin. During these periods, features such as watchtowers, gates, and garrisons were added or enhanced, and the wall's design was unified. Other dynasties also worked on the wall. They repaired its long-standing fortifications, helping this monument to Chinese civilization survive centuries of erosion from use, wind, and weather.

The Great Wall at Jiayuguan

English missionary Mildred Cable traveled through the Gobi Desert, Asia's largest desert, in the 1930s by horse and cart. She wrote of her encounter with the Great Wall at Jiayuguan:

The cart bumped mercilessly over the loose stones of the dismal plain, and each slow mile brought the outline of the fort into clear relief. It was an impressive structure. To the north of the central arch was a turreted watchtower, and from it the long line of the Wall dipped into a valley, climbed a hill and vanished over the summit. The massive monument now towered overhead, and impressive though it was in its own dignity, it made a yet further appeal to the imagination, for this was [Jiayuguan], the Barrier to the Pleasant Valley, the barrier which marks the western end of that amazing and absurd structure known as the Great Wall of China. . . . The length of the Wall, which outlined the crest of the hill to the north, would continue irrespective of difficulties caused by mountains or valleys, rivers and deserts, until it reached the sea 1,400 miles away.[1]

MODERN ATTRACTION

Today, China is in many ways very different from the country it was centuries, or even decades, ago. Imperial rule lasted until 1911 when the last emperor was dethroned as part of a revolt. The former empire's official name is now the People's Republic of China. The capital city of Beijing is a center of commerce and trade. Beijing was also host of the 2008 Summer Olympics. The landscape is a mixture of old and new. But China's modernization does not minimize or erase its rich history or people's appreciation of it. Skyscrapers reach toward the sky as ancient monuments are visited, studied, and enjoyed.

The Great Wall survives today, more than two millennia—2,000 years—after its initial construction. But it no longer serves as a method of defense or to keep China and its people isolated from the rest of

China's Geography

China's landscape is diverse. Mountains tower in the west, and high plateaus lead to rolling hills in central China. The east has plains, lowlands, and great river basins. Deserts and steppes mark the northwest, while mountains dominate the northeast. China's most populous region is the subtropical lowlands of the southeast.

China's weather is as varied as its topography. Bitter cold marks the windswept plateaus of north-central China. The heat is unbearable at times in the tiny strip of land in the tropical south that borders Laos and Vietnam. The northeast enjoys a temperate climate with hot summers and cold winters.

the world. To the contrary, the Great Wall attracts thousands of visitors each day, many of them from other nations. It has become one of the most visited and most recognizable monuments in the world.

The Great Wall is undeniably one of humankind's most prominent and enduring structural feats. It is testament to a people's ability to plan, organize, create, and work diligently. The Great Wall of China is a monument to the Chinese civilization—one that came at great costs and through countless sacrifices. ⌐

World Heritage Site

The United Nations Educational, Scientific and Cultural Organization (UNESCO) designated the Great Wall a World Heritage Site in 1987. Through the work of its World Heritage Centre, UNESCO "seeks to encourage the identification, protection and preservation of cultural and natural heritage around the world considered to be of outstanding value to humanity." UNESCO strives to achieve this goal by advocating "participation of the local population in the preservation of their cultural and natural heritage." UNESCO also promotes "international cooperation in the conservation of our world's cultural and natural heritage."[2]

Beijing's skyline is a mixture of old and new.

Chapter 2

The ancient peoples of China settled along rivers. Most lived near the Yellow River, the Yangtze River, and the West River.

ANCIENT CHINA

The Great Wall of China reflects much of China's extensive history. The nation's roots extend back thousands of years—as early as prehistoric times. China is home to one of the world's oldest continuous civilizations.

The first people reached the area we know as China approximately 50,000 years ago, during the Stone Age. These people survived by hunting and gathering. They lived in caves and used crude tools made of rock and bone. These hunter-gatherers lived a nomadic life, traveling the land in search of food.

A great change occurred when some of these early people began farming and raising animals. Around 10,000 BCE, in the area we know today as China, tribes of ancient people settled mostly along rivers in the north including the Yellow River, the Yangtze River, and the West River. Soil along rivers is fertile, which makes it good for farming. The rivers provided the water necessary for the survival of the people and their crops and animals. By 5000 BCE, the Yellow River valleys contained farming villages. Inhabitants kept animals such as

Civilization and Rivers

Rivers played an important part in the development of Chinese civilization. Other civilizations also developed along rivers in areas beyond China, including the Nile in Egypt and the Indus in Pakistan. Mesopotamia is often referred to as the cradle of civilization because it is considered the location of the oldest known civilization. The name Mesopotamia is Greek for "the land between the two rivers," which refers to the area's location between the Euphrates and Tigris rivers. Today, the area is occupied by Iraq and Syria.

dogs, pigs, and sheep, and they grew crops of millet, wheat, and barley.

However, not all people in ancient China farmed. The region's varied landscape promoted equally varied methods of survival. For people living in drier areas, farming was less likely because the soil simply was not suited to growing crops. China's steppes provided dry grassland that was suitable for grazing. Some of the inhabitants settled but remained hunters and gatherers, living south of the steppes. People living in the steppes tended to be horse riders who maintained a nomadic lifestyle.

THE NEED FOR WALLS

The nomads and farmers led very different lives. The nomads traveled the land in search of food for themselves and grass on which their animals could graze. Farmers remained in a single location to grow and harvest food. They stored the

Different Geography and Climate

China's geography has changed since the Neolithic era (10,000–2000 BCE). There were lakes and marshes to the north and a giant lake in the center. The climate was also different. It was warm and humid. Today, China is colder and drier.

Some of the ancient nomadic peoples in the area known as China changed their lives drastically by settling and farming.

extra food to consume once the growing season was complete, until the next planting season. Farmers often had food readily available, while nomads did not. Stores of grain made farmers and their villages attractive to nomads, who began invading to take the food.

But nomads were not the only invaders farmers and villagers faced. Neighbors also attacked. In order to protect themselves and their highly coveted stores of food, farmers and their villages began to build walls. Although they would not necessarily keep out invaders, the walls slowed down attackers. This gave villagers time to defend themselves against invaders or to run to safety. Over time, these early walls would grow with the villages they surrounded to become a method of defense for different regions in early China.

The Xianyun and the Zhou

A poem from the ninth century BCE tells of a major fight between the Zhou and the Xianyun, a tribe from the north:

In the sixth month all was bustle and excitement.

The war-chariots had been made ready . . .

The Xianyun were in blazing force,

There was no time to lose.

The king had ordered the expedition

To deliver the royal kingdom.[1]

DYNASTIC RULE BEGINS

China's many small settlements developed into self-governing city-states. Different city-states often fought for control of local resources and regional dominance. Leadership was determined by violence. Eventually, the Xia dynasty came to power in the twenty-second century BCE. The Xia dynasty was China's first dynasty, although its existence has been debated. The establishment of the Xia dynasty (circa 2100s–1600s BCE) marked the beginning of a change in Chinese society. There was now a social division with the emergence of a governing class exercising authority over the governed.

The Shang dynasty (circa 1650–1027 BCE) followed the Xia. It is the first dynasty verified by scientists. This dynasty established rule in central and northeastern China. Archaeologists have unearthed a variety of bronze items from the period, including bells, tools, urns, and weapons. The Shang also left behind inscribed animal bones and tortoise shells that have helped scholars understand what life was like during the Shang dynasty. The economy was based primarily on agriculture.

Fact or Fiction?

Not all historians agree that the Xia dynasty was China's first historical dynasty. Many historians believe the Xia dynasty is simply part of Chinese mythology—it is a story told as part of Chinese history. There have long been oral histories in China of the Xia, but there has not been tangible archaeological evidence that the Xia truly existed. That is, not until 1959. Archaeologists excavating in the city of Yanshi uncovered what they believe was probably a capital of the Xia dynasty. Archaeologists have learned that the people at the site were direct ancestors of the Lungshan, early people of China's eastern plains, and predecessors of the Shang. Carbon dating indicates that the people at the site existed from 2100 to 1800 BCE. However, this information has not persuaded many historians to consider the Xia dynasty anything more than myth, and it has not been universally accepted as historical. Instead of the Xia, the Shang dynasty is most often considered China's first historical dynasty.

The Search for Meaning

Two of China's greatest intellectual traditions emerged during the Spring and Autumn and Warring States periods: Confucianism and Taoism, or Daoism. Confucianism emphasizes virtue and duty. The movement's founder, Confucius (551–479 BCE), stressed the importance of human goodness, duty, and doing the best one can. Confucius believed that people could live in harmony if they were kind and did their best.

Daoism focuses on naturalness and the balance of all things. Chinese for "path" or "the way," dao "refers to a power which envelops, surrounds and flows through all things, living and non-living. The Tao, or Dao, regulates natural processes and nourishes balance in the Universe. It embodies the harmony of opposites . . . no love without hate, no light without dark, no male without female."[2]

Peasant farmers supported the kings and nobles who ruled from towns and cities that were walled. However, the Shang rulers were not invincible. The Shang dynasty was overthrown, and the Zhou dynasty (circa 1027–221 BCE) was established. Lasting more than 750 years, the Zhou was China's longest dynasty. To help manage the empire, the Zhou established a feudal-style system in which lords ruled peasant farmers. Long ramparts were constructed during this time. These extended walls protected entire states or regions.

Initially, Zhou rulers were mighty. However, during the latter half of the dynasty, they were figureheads with little power. As the Zhou dynasty declined, lords from several states fought for overall control. This part of the dynasty is divided into two periods: the Spring and Autumn period (770–476 BCE) and the Warring States period (circa 475–

This bronze water pitcher was created during the Zhou dynasty.

221 BCE). During the Spring and Autumn period, lords continued to pledge allegiance to the king and fought amongst themselves. Rival lords attacked each other using chariots, cavalry, and foot soldiers.

The fighting continued during the Warring States period. Lords from seven major city-states fought for control of the entire region: Chu, Han, Qi, Qin, Wei, Yan, and Zhao. Although it was a time of great conflict in China, not all was negative during this time. There was an explosion of philosophical

**Chinese Names
in English**

There are multiple systems for converting Chinese into English. The U.S. government officially adopted the pinyin system more than 20 years ago. The system is also used by the United Nations. Another conversion system is Wade-Giles. These systems result in variations in the English spellings of Chinese names. For example, the first Qin emperor is Qin Shi Huangdi in pinyin and Ch'in-shih Huang Ti and Ch'in Shih Huang-ti in Wade-Giles.

learning as people struggled to find meaning amid the political chaos, war, and suffering of this violent period. Qin was the westernmost state. Qin armies began taking over areas of neighboring states, including Zhou, which was home to the Zhou dynasty. After more than 250 years of fighting, a single state emerged victorious over the others. Eventually, the Qin armies overtook all of Qin's rival states. The Warring States period lasted for more than 200 years. It ended with the unification of China and the establishment of the nation's first emperor. It was the beginning of China's imperial era.

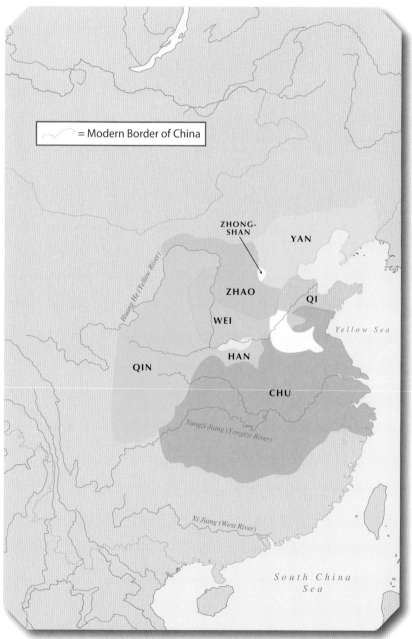

= Modern Border of China

ZHONG-
SHAN

YAN

Huang He (Yellow River)

ZHAO

QI

WEI

Yellow Sea

HAN

QIN

CHU

Yangzi Jiang (Yangtze River)

Xi Jiang (West River)

South China
Sea

*During the Warring States period, China was divided into
several city-states.*

Emperors of later dynasties lived in the Forbidden City in Beijing, China.

IMPERIAL AND MODERN
CHINA

hao Zheng was born in 259 BCE to a prince named Zichu, who was the middle of approximately 20 sons of the king of Qin, one of China's seven major city-states. Because he was a middle son, Zichu was not the immediate heir to the throne of Qin. However, through bribery, Zichu became heir to the throne in 250 BCE. Upon succeeding his father, Zichu ruled for four years as King Zhaoxiang. When Zichu died, Zhao Zheng became king of Qin in 246 or 247 BCE. He was 14 years old. One by one, Zhao Zheng conquered Qin's rival states. When Qi, the final kingdom, was conquered in 221 BCE, Zhao Zheng had unified China. To put himself in a position higher than the kings, princes, and lords that existed in Qin and the conquered states, Zhao Zheng gave himself the title of emperor. He took the name Qin Shi Huangdi, Chinese for "first emperor of Qin." He became the first emperor of China, and the Qin dynasty began.

Shi Huangdi united what were once many states and their various ruling families into a single state with one ruler: Shi Huangdi. His establishment of imperial rule marked a form of government in China that would last more than 2,000 years. Emperors from several dynasties would rule the vast area until the end of the last imperial dynasty in the early twentieth century.

Emperors' Names

In Chinese, *Huangdi* means "emperor," and *Shi* means "first." Therefore, Qin Shi Huangdi means "First Emperor of the Qin." The shorter form *Di* also means emperor, so Wu Di means "Emperor Wu."

The Han dynasty (206 BCE–220 CE) followed
the Qin. Emperors of the Han dynasty followed
the precedent set
by the Qin and
governed through a
national system of
government. But
this unification
of China
would not last.
Instead, the Han
fragmented into
three kingdoms
that occupied the
continent for
much of the third
century CE: Shu,
Wei, and Wu.
The period of the
Three Kingdoms
was followed by
the period of the
Northern and
Southern dynasties.
During this time,

China's First Emperor

As Zhao Zheng fought and defeated Qin's rival city-states, he refused to allow his defeated rivals to rule their home kingdoms as his vassals, or subordinates. Rather, Zheng ruled all of China as sole ruler—as emperor, not merely a king. The princes, dukes, and counts in the other kingdoms lost their titles and privileges, and all of China was divided into 36 provinces, not according to traditional kingdoms. Each of the provinces was ruled by a minister selected by Zheng, now Shi Huangdi, the emperor. The 36 ministers had no right to pass their titles along to their sons, which had once been the practice. Instead, new ministers were subject to appointment and oversight by the emperor. Although China had long been ruled by a number of kings and princes, now all power in the nation flowed from the one emperor who had no equals.

Shi Huangdi was a controversial ruler. He unified China and oversaw the construction of the first Great Wall and a network of roads across the Chinese interior. While the emperor's construction projects helped unify China and the Chinese, these massive building projects cost thousands of lives. In addition, Shi Huangdi outlawed Confucianism, the popular philosophy of the time, and censored his people by banning and burning books that he did not approve.

numerous small and relatively short-lived kingdoms were scattered over the landscape. Reunification occurred in 589 under the Sui dynasty (589–618 CE).

After reunification, China became a world power during the Tang dynasty (618–907 CE). The empire expanded to the north, south, and west when Tang soldiers defeated the Vietnamese, the Tibetans, and the Turks. And culture flourished as music, literature, and other arts advanced. However, this period of growth ended briefly when China was once again divided into northern and southern regions during the Five Dynasties (907–960 CE) in the north and Ten Kingdoms (907–979 CE) in the south. The two periods are often referred to collectively as a single period: Five Dynasties and Ten Kingdoms (907–960 CE). Reunification occurred under the Song dynasty (960–1279 CE). During this dynasty, the Chinese made great strides in science and technology, and the arts were also highly valued. In addition, the government instituted the use of paper money.

Ancient Noodles

In 2005, archaeologists digging at Lajia in north-western China discovered an unusual artifact: a bowl of noodles. The noodles date to about 2000 BCE and provide the earliest evidence of noodles in culinary history. Prior to this discovery, the earliest mention of noodles was a cookbook from the Eastern Han dynasty (25–220 CE). The long, thin noodles discovered in 2005 were made of two kinds of millet.

Mongolian horsemen pursue enemies.

In the early 1200s, the Mongols, a tribe of
barbarians from the north, took over an area in
northern China. Genghis Khan was leader of the
Mongols and began an era of Mongol rule in China.
He ruled China for 12 years. Following Genghis
Khan's death, grandson Kublai Khan eventually took
power. He defeated the Song dynasty and established
the Yuan dynasty in 1279, but this foreign dynasty
lasted less than a century. The Chinese drove the
Mongols out of China and established the Ming

dynasty in 1368. Ming emperors made Beijing, located in the north, the capital of China, moving it from Nanjing in the south. As with the Song dynasty, culture flourished during the Ming dynasty, which is famous for its arts and crafts.

The Ming proved to be the last native Chinese dynasty. It was replaced in 1644 by the Manchu, or Qing, dynasty (1644–1911 CE). This was a foreign dynasty and also China's last dynasty. The Manchus were from an area to the north and northeast of China proper. The Qing government was overthrown in 1911. The emperor, Henry Pu Yi, stepped down in 1912, and more than 2,000 years of imperial rule came to an end.

CHINA: 1912–PRESENT

When the last emperor gave up his throne, the Republic of China was established. But China's new government lasted only a few decades. It fell apart after invasion, war, and internal strife. A civil war in the late 1940s was won by communists who established the People's Republic of China in 1949. People's Republic of

One Person, Many Names

Chinese emperors often had multiple names, such as a family name, a reign title, a temple name, and honorary titles. For example, Emperor Wu of the Han dynasty had the following names: Liu (family name) Che (given name), Tong (courtesy name used by educated Chinese instead of the given name), Han Wu Di (reign name), and Wudi (temple name).

Many Dialects

Centuries-old cultural distinctions are evident today in the Chinese language. There are ten dialect groups. Mandarin, Wu, Cantonese, Min, Xiang, Hakka, and Gan are the traditional main groups. Jin, Hiu, and Ping are more recent classifications that are offshoots of the traditional groups.

China remains the country's official name. This government is still in place.

Although the nomads and emperors of China's past are only memories, there remains an abundance of evidence of the country's rich history. One of the greatest monuments to China's history is the Great Wall.

Development of the China we know today took place over thousands of years and under the rule of many leaders: lords, dukes, kings, and emperors. Their rules and standards, and the cultural and scientific developments that occurred, shaped Chinese life and ultimately helped shape the world. One development that solidified Chinese civilization and unified the Chinese people was the wall, particularly the Great Wall. The mighty structure that has so greatly affected Chinese history began as an idea of a single person: Shi Huangdi.

Chinese Dynasties and Political Periods

2000s–circa 1600s BCE	Xia Dynasty
ca. 1650–ca. 1027 BCE	Shang Dynasty
ca. 1027–221 BCE	Zhou Dynasty
221–206 BCE	Qin Dynasty
206 BCE–220 CE	Han Dynasty
220–589	Three Kingdoms and Northern and Southern Dynasties
589–618	Sui Dynasty
618–907	Tang Dynasty
907–960	Five Dynasties (North)
907–979	Ten Kingdoms (South)
960–1126	Song Dynasty
1127–1279	Southern Song Dynasty
1279–1368	Mongol Yuan Dynasty
1368–1644	Ming Dynasty
1644–1911	Qing Dynasty
1912–1949	Republic of China
1949–present	People's Republic of China

Qin Shi Huangdi, China's first emperor

UNIFYING A NATION

ecoming emperor in 221 BCE made
Shi Huangdi China's most powerful
person. As leader, he made many changes. Shi
Huangdi helped further the development of China
and Chinese civilization by standardizing currency,

laws, weights and measures, and a writing system. Many of the standardizations that Shi Huangdi created helped business, including trading. Standardizing currency also made collecting taxes easier, which benefited the emperor.

Not all of Shi Huangdi's changes benefited his people. Some scholars criticized the emperor in writing. Shi Huangdi ordered the burning of such books. Only a few books about agriculture, fortune-telling, and medicine were spared. This made him unpopular with some Chinese. The emperor was so unpopular with some people that two attempts were made to assassinate him. Shi Huangdi survived both attempts and remained in power.

Shi Huangdi wanted to keep his power. Defending China against invaders would help him remain emperor. Barbarians to the north were the greatest threat to China.

Friendly Nomads

Shi Huangdi wished to maintain communities of friendly nomads beyond the wall to serve as a first line of defense against attackers. These friendly nomads became increasingly like the Chinese in their culture and language. Frequently, they crossed over the wall to settle in Chinese lands. This was unacceptable to the emperors. Although these groups spoke Chinese and practiced Chinese customs, they were not truly Chinese. Eventually, the friendly nomads became more of a threat than the more savage nomads of the far north. Most of the invaders who threatened imperial China were not savage barbarians but groups of other ethnicities who were Chinese in terms of their language and cultural practices.

A series of walls already existed in the north. Shi Huangdi wanted to link these walls to create a single wall to defend his empire's northern border.

FOREIGNERS OUT, CHINESE IN

Shi Huangdi's idea for a wall along China's northern border was intended to be more than a means for keeping foreigners out of his land. It would keep the Chinese people in China. The wall project would also provide employment to the thousands of disbanded soldiers who had formerly been engaged in inter-state warfare. A massive wall along the northern border would keep the Chinese separated from foreigners who were considered inferior and keep them free from the influence of other peoples. It would also give the emperor greater power over his people in the north by allowing him to control trade between Chinese and tribes beyond the wall.

The Legend of General Nan Chung

A poem from the seventh century BCE tells of an ancient time when a legendary king ordered his general, Nan Chung, to build a wall to help defend the kingdom from an otherworldly foe:

*The King charged Nan Chung
To go and build a wall in the [disturbed] region
How numerous were his chariots!
How splendid his dragon, his tortoise and serpent flags!
The son of Heaven had charged us
To build a wall in that northern region.
Awe-inspiring was Nan Chung;
The Heen-yun [Xienyun] were sure to be swept away.[1]*

In certain parts of Asia, the nomadic lifestyle that existed in Asia centuries ago continues today. Here, two young Mongolian nomad children are tending their herd.

Shi Huangdi convinced his people that barbarians from the north were threatening China's newfound peace and prosperity. He said that attack was imminent and that they had to act quickly to prevent the barbarians from overrunning China. He proposed linking the walls of the former states of the Qin, Yan, and Zhao of the Warring States period. Shi Huangdi also proposed expanding the wall so that it would stretch from the Yellow Sea westward

Promenade of Qin Shi Huangdi *is a painting on silk from the Qing dynasty.*

more than 1,500 miles (2,414 km) to the city of Jiayuguan on the edge of the Gobi Desert.

The emperor's proposed wall would link the interior of his new empire. A project of such immense size would require the mobilization of hundreds of thousands—if not millions—of men, tens of thousands of work animals, millions of tons of equipment and supplies, and accommodations for the architects and commanders of the project. In addition, roads would have to be built in order to deliver the abundance of supplies needed for the construction project.

Linking the existing ramparts into a single wall and then expanding that wall would help unite previously warring communities. Supplies and resources would be transported from one territory to another, and men from various regions would work side by side. Building the Great Wall was not entirely a defensive effort. It was an attempt to foster a sense of national identity rather than local or regional identities. Old barriers— physical and cultural—that separated people and lands within China would

Walling Oneself In

Surrounding their town or city with a wall helped villagers protect their settlement. Invaders would have to find a way over, around, or even under the wall. Meanwhile, defenders could take positions on top of the wall and attack their opponents with arrows, spears, stones, roof tiles, and cauldrons of boiling oil or molten lead. As the methods of combat advanced, walls became higher, thicker, and more elaborate.

be demolished by Shi Huangdi's wall project, the
Wall of Qin.

Defining an Empire's Border

The Wall of Qin would be built along a
line across China between the nomad-friendly
steppes—land unsuitable for agriculture but good
for grazing—and the zone of civilized agriculture,
where farmers tended the land. The wall would
mark the point beyond which the Chinese emperor
and his government would cease to rule. The Wall
of Qin would serve as the "outer limit of desirable
expansion" for the Chinese emperor, keeping the
Chinese in regions where agriculture was possible
and out of the harsher nomad zone.[2] The Chinese
would live south of the wall on land suitable for
farming. Nomads would live north of the wall on
land appropriate for nomadic herding.

As China's first emperor, Shi Huangdi
envisioned great things for himself. If his wall
succeeded in being built, it would help him create
a strong land and a unified people. For this to
happen, the emperor's plans had to be put into
action. In a matter of a few years, the Wall of Qin
would move quickly from idea to reality. To do that,

the Chinese would need great organization, steady leadership, and countless resources.

Construction of the Wall of Qin would become a triumph of domestic policy. It would bring together peoples who were once at odds with one another. New roads would be built for the project that would allow free passage between lands that were recently separate kingdoms. The project would stimulate the unified Chinese economy and inspire a wealth of poems and

Terra-Cotta Army

In 1974, a farmer near Xian in north-central China stumbled upon what would become one of China's greatest archaeological finds. He found a nearly intact army of terra-cotta soldiers at least 2,000 years old. This army, made out of baked clay, was stationed near the mausoleum, or tomb, of Shi Huangdi. In addition to building his wall, the emperor forced some 700,000 convicts to build a mausoleum. Many of the workers were killed upon completion of the project to keep its location a mystery.

The army was excavated and put on display in a museum built at the excavation site in 1975. The massive army includes approximately 8,000 life-size figures representing generals, footmen, horsemen, and horses in battle formation. No two figures are alike. Each is highly detailed with its own pose, armor, hairstyle, and facial expression. Each figure was once painted and held real weapons. The paint faded with time, and the weapons had been stolen, but many of the soldiers have been restored to their original splendor.

Archaeologists continue to work at the excavation site. The Museum of the Terra-Cotta Warriors and Horses of Qin Shihuang has become a popular tourist destination. In 1987, the United Nations Educational, Scientific, and Cultural Organization listed the mausoleum of Shi Huangdi, including the terra-cotta warriors, as a World Heritage Site.

legends. Shi Huangdi's wall would become a symbol of unity and strength. However, the project would bring together workers in the worst conditions, and many of them would suffer and die while working to complete Shi Huangdi's wall. Poems about the wall attest to this. The wall became known among the people as "The Longest Cemetery on Earth." Building the Wall of Qin was a great success, but it was also a project that caused great hardship for the Chinese. ⌒

Great Wall of Mexico

Some U.S. politicians advocate building a fence along the United States–Mexico border to decrease the number of Mexican immigrants entering the United States illegally. Also referred to as the Great Wall of Mexico, the proposed fence would stretch across mountains, deserts, and rivers. If built, the wall will be approximately 2,000 miles (3,200 km) long and cost hundreds of millions of dollars to complete.

Statues of a horse and a soldier from Shi Huangdi's terra-cotta army.

*Remains of the westernmost tower of the Great Wall
near Jiayuguan, China*

BUILDING THE
WALL OF QIN

Shi Huangdi's wall project was massive. The approximately 1,800 miles (2,900 km) of the Wall of Qin were built in three segments. The first segment was erected to run west roughly 800 miles (1,290 km) from the Yellow Sea to the Yellow

River. The second segment was constructed to stretch 600 miles (966 km) from the Yellow River's eastern arm to the city of Liangchow. The third segment, about 450 miles (724 km), was built to connect Liangchow to Jiayuguan in the Gobi Desert.

ORGANIZING CONSTRUCTION

Construction of the Wall of Qin was supervised by the emperor's most trusted general, Meng Tian. The general organized 34 supply bases across China along the route of the proposed wall. These supply bases were the headquarters of the wall's engineers and housed soldiers. They were also essential to nourish the workforce, as the terrain through which the wall passed was not good for farming. Incredible amounts of resources were needed for the project and those working on it. Huge caravans of food and supplies were marched from the Chinese interior along imperial highways that were built for the project. The supply

Qin Wall Legends

There are several legends about Shi Huangdi and his wall. According to one legend, the emperor rode on a magic horse across all of China. The horse stomped his hooves every 9 or 10 miles (14 or 16 km), and a watchtower sprang up every place the horse stomped.

Another legend says that no fewer than nine suns created by the emperor himself lit up the sky while the Great Wall was being built so that the men could work night and day and always in dry weather.

Meng Tian

Meng Tian descended from a long line of great military generals and architects. He was a talented general who won many victories for Shi Huangdi. Meng Tian was also hardworking and well organized.

In addition to serving a splendid military career and orchestrating the construction of the initial Great Wall of China, Meng Tian is also credited with inventing the writing brush. His image can be found today in the stalls of brush sellers across China. He is considered a semidivine patron of writers and brush makers. However, it is unlikely that Meng Tian invented the writing brush. Images of writing brushes can be traced back to 1500 BCE, long before he was born. Rather than inventing the writing brush, Meng Tian probably improved the writing brush or simply introduced it to the more remote areas of China.

bases were the starting points for construction.

Building the wall required a lot of organization. Meng Tian oversaw dozens of commanders. Each of these men managed hundreds of low-level officers who, in turn, supervised thousands of workers.

The Workers

Wall workers came from throughout China. Most of the empire's male population was ordered to work on the emperor's project, regardless of social status. Hundreds of thousands of men were ordered as part of their military service to build the emperor's wall. Peasants and farmers also toiled on the project. Shi Huangdi forced more than 500,000 men from farming villages and towns across China to build his wall. He also pressed intellectuals into service. Criminals worked on the wall as well.

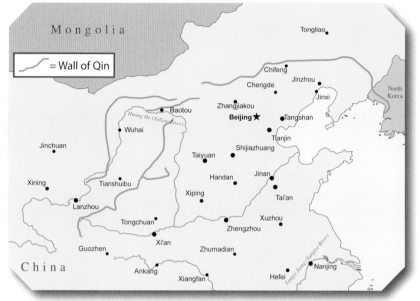

The Wall of Qin joined many of China's small walls. It created a great defensive structure along the country's northern border.

Wall workers did not have an easy life. Guarded by soldiers, they worked as long as there was daylight. Just as in society at large, there was a class system among those who worked on the wall. The men who had been taken from prisons to work on the project had a particularly difficult time. They were easy to identify: their heads had been shaved and their faces made black. In addition, these men had to wear chains while working.

Man-made Wall

According to legend, 400,000 men died while building the Wall of Qin. Construction pressed on at such an amazing rate that men who fell into the wall were often entombed within it. They were crushed between giant rocks or buried beneath mounds of stone or earth because saving the men would have slowed production. This ode from the Qin period reflects the sacrifice involved in creating the Wall of Qin:

If you have a son, don't
raise him.
If you have a girl, feed
her dried meat.
Can't you see, the Long
Wall
Is propped up on
skeletons.[1]

Workers lived where they worked. There were camps along the wall, but they were inadequate in both quantity and quality. There simply was not enough shelter for the many workers, and the available housing provided little protection from the elements. The workers also went without beds and blankets. As a result, many of the men slept on the ground without shelter.

Getting food and drink was also a challenge for workers. When construction took place near a water source such as a river or lake, the men had fresh water. However, when working in a location where there was no river or lake, the workers had no fresh water to drink.

As with the supply of water, there often was not enough food. The reason was twofold. First, the entire empire suffered a shortage of food because the farmers and peasants who usually worked the land and produced food were now working on the wall and other projects ordered by Shi Huangdi, including new roads and canals. Second, what little food was sent along supply routes to the workers was often taken by bandits. Workers who toiled on the Wall of Qin worked hard, long hours for nothing in return—not even the basics needed to survive. Nevertheless, construction proceeded.

MANY TOWERS

Construction of the Wall of Qin headed east and west from each of Meng Tian's 34 supply bases. Garrison towers were built first.

The Story of Meng Chiang Nu

Chinese folklore tells of Meng Chiang Nu, a beautiful maiden, and Fan San-lang, a scholar. The couple married, and Fan San-lang was drafted to work on the wall.

After many months, Fan San-lang's ghost visited Meng Chiang Nu and told her he was freezing and growing weak. The young woman went to find her love. A god took her to the construction site. Workmen explained that Fan San-lang was buried in the wall. She prayed that she might give her husband a proper burial. The gods split open the wall, exposing thousands of bones. Meng Chiang Nu dripped blood from her finger onto the bones to determine which belonged to her husband. It dribbled off the bones of strangers but seeped into the bones of her love.

The grieving wife left with her husband's bones. On her journey home, the emperor passed by. He was struck by her beauty and wanted to make her a lady of the court. If she refused, Meng Chiang Nu would be executed for damaging the wall. She hated the emperor but agreed to marry him if he presided over a state funeral for her husband at the ocean. The emperor agreed. After Fan San-lang's bones were scattered in the water and the service ended, Meng Chiang Nu threw herself into the sea to avoid marrying the emperor and to reunite with her husband's spirit.

These massive brick-and-stone structures were erected every few miles to house hundreds of guards who would be at the ready should an attack occur.

Tall watchtowers were built between the garrison towers. They were spaced every few hundred yards so that no section of the wall would be out of range of archers stationed atop the watchtowers. Expert archers were protected by bastions and battlements at the top of each tower. These marksmen were trained to strike any invader approaching the wall by shooting arrows through slits in the walls.

The watchtowers were close enough to enable coverage of the wall from all angles. They were approximately 39 feet (12 m) high. The base was 39 feet (12 m) across and narrowed toward the top to approximately 30 feet (9 m). From atop the watchtowers, fires could be lit to notify the soldiers at the garrison towers of approaching invaders.

Connecting the Towers

The towers were joined by sections of wall. These sections were at least 20 feet (6 m) high and wide enough for eight men to march abreast, or side by side, in formation. The wall was constructed using the *hangtu* method. *Hangtu* is Chinese for "tamped earth." Using this method, a frame was created from wood or bamboo. The frame held dirt that workers dumped in and then packed down to remove air pockets. Packing down the earth made it very strong. After packing down the earth, more dirt would be dumped into the frame and packed down, creating layers. The process of layering and packing down was repeated until the wall became the desired height. Once this height was reached, the frame was removed and moved to create the next section of the wall.

Warning Signals

Guards stationed in the towers along the wall and in the lookout towers north of the wall used fire and smoke to communicate: smoke during the day and fire during the night. Signals were sent following a specific code. A single fire or smoke signal meant 100 attackers. Two signals meant 500 attackers. Three signals meant more than 1,000 attackers. Four signals meant 5,000 attackers. Five signals meant the worst: 10,000 attackers.

The materials used to build the wall varied according to the surrounding terrain. For example, the mountainous segment of the wall that runs from the Yellow Sea to the westernmost arm of the Yellow River was made using stone and brick in addition to using dirt. In the Ordos region, the second leg of the wall was also constructed with bricks and wood. In the Gobi Desert, the wall was built using gravel, sand, and twigs. Sections of the Wall of Qin made from twigs and pebbles still exist.

Equivalent Distance

If it were built in the United States today, the Wall of Qin would stretch from Los Angeles, California, to Atlanta, Georgia.

BUILDING NORTH OF CHINA

The Wall of Qin project included more than the initial Great Wall. Construction extended north of the empire into barbarian territory. Beyond the Wall of Qin, some 15,000 freestanding lookout towers were erected and stocked with enough provisions to withstand a siege of up to four months. Guards stationed in these towers served as an early warning system. They sent signals to the Great Wall notifying soldiers of any approaching enemies.

The Wall of Qin was completed in 214 BCE. It was nearly 2,000 miles (3,200 km) long with more than 25,000 towers and took seven years to build. Thousands of Chinese participated in its construction and died during the process. The project stood as a testament to the power of the newly united China and its emperor, but the Chinese suffered greatly in the building of the first Great Wall. Others would work to maintain and expand the Wall of Qin centuries after the end of the Qin dynasty. ⌐

A stretch of unreconstructed wall, framed by the crumbling window of a tower at the Simatai section of the Great Wall

Chapter
6

Trade increased during Han rule. A camel caravan travels the famous Silk Road trade route.

THE WALL AFTER QIN: 206 BCE—1368 CE

Shi Huangdi died in 210 BCE. The Qin dynasty ended in 206 BCE when people from China's Han region took power and established the Han dynasty. Han emperors would rule the great empire for more than four centuries.

China prospered during the Han dynasty. Under the Qin emperors, the Chinese people suffered greatly. In contrast, the Han emperors focused on people. Art and philosophy thrived. Elements of Chinese culture spread to nearby regions, including parts of Korea, Mongolia, and Vietnam.

Wu Di's Wall

As China thrived overall, the Wall of Qin deteriorated. In part, this was the result of neglect. Unhappy with the project and short on money, the Chinese stopped working on it. Moreover, much of the wall was left empty, free of soldiers, for the next century. The Great Wall fell into disrepair throughout the next 100 years.

Assuming power in 141 BCE at the age of 15, Wu was the seventh Han emperor. Because of his young age, he was managed by royal advisors until becoming an adult. Emperor Wu, or Wu Di, would rule for more than 50 years. Chinese for "martial emperor," Wu Di used his armies to fight nomadic tribes who threatened China's borders. But Wu Di relied on

The Han People

The Han dynasty is so revered that the people of China today refer to themselves as the Han People.

more than troops and military planning as emperor. He was also a diplomatic leader. His use of both military force and political skill brought Wu Di and China great power. During his rule, the empire doubled in size, and Wu Di exercised influence over much of East Asia. In addition to expanding the empire, Wu Di proposed extending the Great Wall. The Han emperors focused on trading with peoples to the west. Extending the wall westward would expand protection along trade routes. Wu Di ordered a 300-mile (483-km) extension of the Great Wall

The Silk Road

Rich in valuable goods and technologies, such as paper and the printing press, China had been trading with Western peoples since at least 1000 BCE. However, from approximately 300 BCE to 1600 CE, goods and ideas traveled westward from China on a series of routes known as the Silk Road.

The name "Silk Road" comes from the most popular and precious item from China: silk. An expensive cloth in the West, silk was prized for its texture and shimmer. Because the silk-making process was a secret, China was the only source of the material for many years.

Caravans of camels and horses carried precious cargos over thousands of miles of trade route. The caravans were safe from attack from bandits while in China, put under the protection of the troops along the Great Wall. But the journey through central Asia was dangerous. The Silk Road wandered through Tibet's highlands, over the mountains of Afghanistan and Pakistan, across the Iranian plain, and on to the Mediterranean Sea. Other routes cut across Russia and through India to the Indian Ocean.

Silk was the most costly and popular commodity carried along the Silk Road. Other prized items included white paper, jade, and bronzes.

westward, including "a beacon every 5 li, a tower every 10 li, a fort every 30 li, and a castle every 100 li."[1]

Wu Di formed a peaceful relationship with the nomads beyond the Great Wall, including the northern people known as the Xiongnu. This action helped create the Silk Road, China's westerly trade route. With peace established, the soldiers stationed along the Great Wall were not needed to defend traders against attacks. Instead, they acted as rule enforcers and gatekeepers. They kept constant watch on the Xiongnu for any suspicious movements and raiding.

Wu Di died in 87 BCE. The peace he established would continue for many more years. Chinese culture thrived. Important inventions were created during the Han dynasty, including a seismograph to detect earthquakes, the wheelbarrow, and a stern rudder that made steering ships easier. Perhaps most important was the creation of paper in 105 CE.

Silk

For centuries, China has been famous for silk. The smooth, soft fabric was developed by the ancient Chinese as early as 6000 BCE. The process of creating silk started in northern China. There, silkworms were fed mulberry leaves. This helped them to molt, or shed their skin, and spin their cocoons. The cocoons were then boiled to kill the worms, which were removed. Raw silk is the thread of silkworm cocoons.

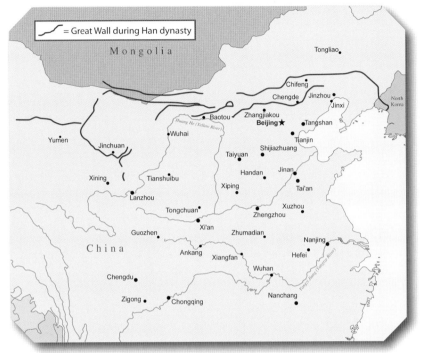

Many dynasties added to the Great Wall. Construction during the Han dynasty provided one of the greatest expansions.

However, while these achievements were taking place, problems in other areas continued. Subsequent Han emperors did not rule as effectively as Wu Di had. Some emperors were poor leaders, and China was simply a difficult nation to oversee because of its size. While the Xiongnu people were now allies, other groups posed threats of invasion. Overseeing and protecting the country became too much for the Han government to manage. After 400 years of ruling over China, the Han dynasty ended in 220 CE.

CHINA AFTER THE HAN

The prosperity the Chinese experienced during Han rule eventually faded, as did the empire's mighty wall. In a matter of decades, by 300 CE, people from the north controlled portions of the Great Wall.

For the next several centuries, other emperors and dynasties ruled China. Different dynasties expanded the wall to varying degrees. The Northern Wei (386–534 CE) added 621 miles (999 km) of wall, the Northern Qi (550–577 CE) added more than 3,300 miles (5,311 km), and the Sui (581–618 CE) added 932 miles (1,500 k). During the Song dynasty (960–1279 CE), threats from the fierce Khitan from the northeast forced a 400-mile (644-km) extension of the Great Wall past Shanhaiguan on the Yellow Sea into Manchuria (located north of present-day North Korea).

DIVIDED AGAIN

Wanyan Aguda was the leader of the Jurchen people in Manchuria, a region that had been incorporated into the Chinese Empire by the Liao dynasty (907–1125 CE). Wanyan Aguda took control of the Chinese-controlled Jurchen territories. His army fought continuously with the Liao troops from 1114 to 1122 in northern China. In 1115, after a series of military successes, Wanyan Aguda proclaimed himself emperor of the Jurchen Jin, or Jin dynasty (1115–1254 CE). In 1122, his army finally defeated the Liao dynasty. The Jin dynasty would rule only northern China. Southern China was under the control of the Southern Song dynasty (1127–1279 CE). China was divided again.

The Song dynasty was firmly in power south of the Huai River and ruled from their capital city of Lin'an. The Song emperors were powerful and prosperous. The Jin emperors were disliked by the Chinese people. The Jin feared the growing power of another non-Chinese group from the north: the Mongols.

"I calculate there are five advantages to building long walls: it will end the problem of mobile defence; the nomads can graze the north, eliminating their need to raid; we can look for the enemy on top of a wall, and no longer have to wait for an attack; it removes anxiety about border defence and the need to mount defence when it is not necessary; it permits the easy transport of supplies and therefore prevents insufficiency."[2]

—*Gao Lü, high-ranking official, Northern Wei dynasty, in a speech in 484 CE*

THE MONGOLS

The Mongols were a loose band of nomadic tribes. Each tribe was ruled by a chieftain. The chieftains elected one of their members to serve as arch chieftain, or khan. In 1162, a boy was born to a tribal chieftain named Yesukai. This boy, Temujin, grew up to be a courageous fighter, skilled horseman, and strong leader. According to legend, at the age of 11, Temujin could ride on horseback without using the reins and shoot dozens of arrows in all directions while riding, without missing a single target.

When Temujin was a boy, his father died. The young warrior tried to claim his father's position as chieftain, but many people stood in his way. Fighting broke out between Temujin's supporters and his rivals. This fighting lasted for years and provided Temujin practice in warfare and tribal politics. After years of fighting, Temujin became tribal chieftain in 1204. He was 37 years old.

In 1206, Temujin was elected khan. He was given the title *Genghis Khan*, which means "universal ruler." Genghis Khan was leader of all the Mongols. He united the disparate, disorganized, and independent tribes of Mongols into a single nation. This resulted in a massive force that allowed him to easily crush

A Divided Society

Not all people were equal in ancient China. Society consisted of four main classes that were regarded with varying levels of respect. Scholars could read and write, so they were held in highest regard. Peasants were the second-highest social class. Peasants held this high position because their hard work provided China with food. Artisans held the third-highest social position. These are the people who made a variety of items by hand, including cooking utensils, tools, and weapons. Merchants were the lowest class. Some Chinese were career soldiers. However, soldiers did not have their own class because they were not regarded highly.

rival nomadic kingdoms throughout central Asia. Genghis Khan earned a reputation as a brilliant leader and a fearsome warrior. By 1211, he subdued all of the peoples between the Mongolian heartland and the Great Wall. He then set his eyes on conquering the vast and rich empire that lay beyond the wall.

As the Mongol threat increased, the Jin rulers began to panic. Hated by the Chinese and targeted by Genghis Khan, the Jin emperors strove to improve the centuries-neglected Great Wall. They also built smaller parallel walls north of the Great Wall watchtowers as an additional line of defense.

KHAN'S INVASION

Genghis Khan knew the Chinese disliked the Jin rulers. He also knew that the Song rulers in southern China were waiting for the right moment to reclaim the north.

Genghis Khan claimed that his only goal in invading China would be to drive out the Jin and free the Chinese people. He claimed the Chinese people would welcome the Mongols as liberators.

Between 1211 and 1214, Genghis Khan led his Mongols over the Great Wall and to the capital city of Yenching (present-day Beijing). Because the Great Wall had been in disrepair, it provided little barrier against invaders, including Genghis Khan and his people. However, he was overwhelmed by Yenching.

The vast city was surrounded by a wall 40 feet (12 m) high with hundreds of immense watchtowers and heavy gates. The wall was encircled by three moats. At each corner of the city, there was a fort of one square mile (2.6 sq km) with its own system of walls, towers, and moats. Should anyone attack, these corner forts had enough supplies to withstand a lengthy siege.

Genghis Khan was ready to give up his attack on Yenching when he learned that the city's residents were prepared to rebel against the Jin rulers. A revolt erupted, and the doors of Yenching were opened to the Mongol leader. In 1215, he became ruler of China north of the Huai River. He would rule for a dozen years.

CHINA REUNITED

Genghis Khan died in 1227. Control of his vast empire passed to his sons. Ogodai ruled the Chinese portion of the empire. The other sons held power over other areas of the empire. In 1241, Genghis Khan's grandson took control of China. He called himself Kublai Khan. In 1264, his Mongol forces defeated the last of the Song emperors in the south. In 1271, Kublai Khan declared himself emperor of all China and the first emperor of the Yuan dynasty (1279–1368 CE). China was united again.

Although unification of China was a triumphant step for Kublai Khan, the fact remained that the Yuan dynasty was not Chinese. The great empire of China was being ruled by people who were not welcome by the Chinese. Following Kublai Khan's death in 1294, the Chinese began to fight for control of their country. After nearly a century of rule by non-Chinese, the Yuan dynasty would come to an end in 1368. A new Chinese dynasty would take power that would launch a massive expansion of the Great Wall in order to keep barbarians out of China.

Genghis Khan led the Mongols to power in China.

A Ming dynasty fortress at Jiayuguan, China, the westernmost limit of the Great Wall

THE MING DYNASTY

Zhu Yuanzhang was born in 1328 in modern Anhwei Province. He was the youngest of four sons. In 1344, a serious famine and diseases took the lives of most of his family members. To survive, Zhu Yuanzhang placed himself under the care of Buddhist monks, which was his father's wish. There, he learned to read, but his studies ended when the monastery could no longer help because it had been destroyed by Mongols or had run out of money. Zhu Yuanzhang left the monastery and spent time begging for food. In the 1350s, he joined a band of rebels and was soon in command after demonstrating a talent for organization and leadership. Zhu Yuanzhang later met and began studying with Confucian scholars. He received an education in state affairs from these scholars and noblemen he met through them.

Zhu Yuanzhang advanced quickly among the rebels with whom he fought the Yuan dynasty. As general of the rebels, he had the support of the noblemen, the scholars, the common people, and a number of important military leaders. He and his rebels defeated the troops of the

Ming Vases

Chinese artisans produced an impressive quality of ceramic ware throughout Chinese imperial history. Some of the most prized ceramics were produced during the Ming dynasty. Craftsmen during the Ming period perfected porcelain vessels with intricate blue glazes using a process that originated in Persia (present-day Iran). Today, Ming vases are very valuable and highly sought by collectors of fine art. In May 2006, one vase from the Ming dynasty sold for more than $10 million at auction.

During the Ming dynasty, the Chinese excelled in pottery. In 2006, the vase shown here was auctioned for a record amount: $10,122,558.

Yuan dynasty in 1368, and he proclaimed himself emperor. Zhu Yuanzhang established the Ming dynasty (1368–1644 CE) and was its first emperor. He chose Hongwu as his reign name.

Under the Hongwu emperor's rule, China experienced a cultural, artistic, and philosophical revival. This was, in large part, due to the fact that the Hongwu emperor returned traditional powers to the Confucian scholar officials. In addition, he again required that government ministers and bureaucrats pass examinations in Confucian literature and philosophy. The use of Mongol styles of dress and the use of Mongol names were outlawed. This contributed to the flourishing of traditional Chinese culture.

The Hongwu emperor brought many changes to China. He established the original Ming capital of Nanjing as the capital of China and reformed China's code of law and updated the military. He also introduced agricultural modernization and promoted farming. These changes ushered in an era of general prosperity and a population boom. The Hongwu emperor helped his homeland become a thriving, wealthy, and mighty empire with a flourishing culture.

A Cultural Rebirth

The Chinese novel developed during the Ming era, evolving from the traditional tales of professional storytellers. The chapters mark the points at which money would have been collected from those enjoying the storytelling. Novels were written in the language of the people rather than the ancient ceremonial language understood by only the educated elite. Some of the best-known Ming novels are still enjoyed today.

Also, many encyclopedias were written that contained detailed information on a variety of subjects, including science, medicine, history, and music. Dictionaries were also published. One dictionary, published in 1615, simplified the Chinese system of writing. The dictionary established the system of 214 radicals or root parts, that form the core of Chinese characters.

AN ERA OF REBUILDING

With China back under Chinese rule, the Hongwu emperor wanted to ensure his country's safety from another invasion. The Mongols had been driven out of China, but they still posed the possibility of invasion. There were also northern tribes that were a threat, including the Dada, the Nuzhen, and the Wala. To help secure the safety of his country and his reign, the Hongwu emperor returned the government's focus to defending China's northern frontier. The Great Wall once again had to serve as defense against attackers. The Hongwu

Yongle's New Capital

The Hongwu emperor's successor was overthrown by an uncle who then became emperor. While emperor, the Yongle emperor (1403–1424 CE) moved China's capital from Nanjing, which means "southern capital," in the south to Dadu in the north. Dadu was once a Mongol city. Because the battle to overthrow the Mongols resulted in widespread devastation of Dadu, the relocation required a massive building campaign that took 16 years to complete. More than 200,000 workers labored on the project. The Yongle emperor inaugurated China's new capital city Beijing, Chinese for "northern capital," on February 2, 1421. It was New Year's Day in China.

Moving the capital city from Nanjing to Beijing was a strategic maneuver. Beijing is located in northern China. To prevent future raids by the Mongols, the Ming emperors decided to reestablish Chinese supremacy over the northern country along the Great Wall. The area had been badly neglected during the previous two dynasties. Basing his entire government in northern China allowed the emperor to keep a close eye on the northern frontier.

emperor contributed to frontier defenses with the fortification of strong points across the north, which served as bases to launch military campaigns.

The Hongwu emperor ruled for 30 years. But his death did not mark the end of refortification of the Great Wall. The wall had been neglected for centuries and would require rebuilding. Reconstruction of China's northern defense would continue long after the Hongwu emperor's reign with subsequent Ming emperors, particularly those in the middle and later years of the dynasty. The greatest amount of construction on the Great Wall occurred during the Ming era.

The Yongle emperor (1403–1424 CE) was the third Ming emperor. He ordered a wall construction project, saying, "At each signal station let the towers be built higher and stronger; within must be laid up food, fuel,

Ming Watchtowers

Ming expansion of the Great Wall included the addition of watchtowers two stories tall. Guards stationed at the towers lived on the first floor and observed the wall and surrounding area from the second floor. In addition to serving as a living space, the first floor was used as a storage space for food and weapons.

The Mutianyu Great Wall, a portion of the wall built during the Ming dynasty that has not been reconstructed

medicine, and weapons for four moons. Beside the tower let a wall be opened, enclosed by a wall as high as the tower itself, presenting the appearance of a double gateway, inner and outer. Be on your guard at all times with anxious care."[1]

A New Design Element

Under the leadership of the Chenghua emperor (1464–1487 CE), the design of the Great Wall was reconfigured to accommodate a new weapon: the cannon. The new Ming wall consisted of a solid brick rampart topped with battlements and parapets. The walls were built 25 feet (8 m) thick, 30 feet (9 m) high, and 15 feet (5 m) across at the top. The stone-and-brick construction was unique to the Great Wall section nearest the capital, Beijing. However, in the west, parts of the wall were restored and rebuilt using the same manner of construction and design that had been used during the Qin dynasty more than 1,000 years earlier.

Fortification of and additions to the Great Wall continued throughout the Ming dynasty. Some portions of the wall were doubled, with two walls running parallel, to increase the Great Wall's ability to defend China against invaders. In addition, passes were added to the wall. Six passes—three inner and three outer—were secured gates that controlled movement into and out of certain areas of China. Other Ming additions to the Great Wall included fortresses, towers, and observation posts. Nine garrisons were built, each one serving as a center for control of its section of the wall. Two more garrisons were added later.

Wanli Chang Cheng

Many people—Chinese and Westerners alike—have associated the Great Wall entirely with the Ming. They incorrectly believed the Wanli emperor was the creator of the Great Wall. The Chinese name for the Great Wall, *Wan-Li Chang Cheng*—"Long Wall of 10,000 li"—was translated to mean "the wall of Wanli."

The monument was perfected during the reign of one of the last Ming emperors, the Wanli emperor (1572–1620 CE). He was responsible for the greatest amount of wall building, including the construction of many of the walls and towers that remain intact today. Constructing the Ming wall was similar in many ways to building the walls during previous dynasties. But there were changes: some made for easier building, while others posed challenges.

A man dressed in a Ming dynasty costume stands at the Great Wall.

A walkway at the Jiayuguan Fort, the Ming fortress that protects the mountain pass at the west end of the Great Wall

A Final Great Expansion

During the Ming dynasty (1368–1644 CE), the Great Wall was extended by more than 4,500 miles (7,200 km). The construction during this period would prove to be the wall's last great expansion. Building was done under the watchful eyes of a group of generals. Each general had a base in a major town along the wall and oversaw thousands of subordinates. In turn, these men supervised numerous laborers. Just as during Shi Huangdi's initial Great Wall construction project, work on the Ming wall required extensive planning and massive resources, including workers.

CONSTRUCTION METHODS

Although many centuries had passed since the initial construction of the Wall of Qin, the hangtu method of wall building was still in use. However, other developments had occurred that made construction during the Ming era easier than previous expansions. The Ming wall was uniform.

The Ming wall was built on foundations of massive blocks of heavy granite as long as 14 feet (4 m) cut from quarries and rolled over logs to be put in place. The granite blocks and clay bricks were all cut to be uniform in size, shape, and color. In the mountainous regions

Gunpowder

Although the Chinese invented gunpowder, the Europeans were the first to make viable weapons out of it. The Chinese did employ gunpowder in battle, and even had early versions of the cannon, but the gunpowder was more often used to set spears on fire.

nearest Nanjing, the entire wall to the battlements was made solely from granite blocks. Elsewhere, the Ming-era construction relied heavily on tiles and bricks. The bricks were made at the building site by peasants who stomped clay, sand, and straw together, and then formed the mixture into blocks. The wet bricks were baked at high temperatures in kilns, or ovens, built specifically for the wall project. The process resulted in millions of bricks, each the same as the next and weighing 22 pounds (10 kg).

Lime is a white powder derived from limestone. It was mixed with sticky rice and sometimes sand to make mortar that cemented the bricks together. The rice was considered the secret ingredient. However, the sheer weight of the stone blocks would have been enough to keep them in place.

The architects working under the Ming emperors followed the course

Making Bricks

To make bricks available to workers without huge transportation costs, brick-making workshops were set up at intervals along the length of the wall. This allowed bricks to be made and baked on site. Not only did this eliminate the need to coordinate transportation, but bricks could also be made to order.

In December 2002, archaeologists in China discovered 48 brick kilns, 24 of which were packed with 5,000 bricks each. The dimensions of the bricks are the same as those of the bricks used to build the Ming sections of the Great Wall.

of natural barriers such as cliffs and rivers with their new wall sections. This saved on labor and building materials. For example, the Ming wall in the mountains near Badaling has a steep drop on its northern side.

Constructing the Ming wall was not easy. Building materials that could not be obtained locally were transported from China's interior by carts drawn by horses or mules. Workers then carried materials up the hills and mountains. Bricks were wrapped in cloth. Lime, sand, and pebbles were placed in wicker baskets. Sometimes, men stood in long lines and passed bricks and stones from one man to the next, one by one. In some of the higher elevations, bricks were tied to the horns of goats that were driven up the side of the mountain. Tools for lifting and carrying heavy bricks and stones included wheelbarrows, levers, ropes, and winches.

Transporting Bricks

While construction methods advanced over time, one method of moving bricks continued throughout the centuries of construction on the Great Wall: workers carried the bricks. In steep terrain, where wagons and donkeys could not go, bricks were loaded onto a wooden shelf and strapped to a worker's back similarly to a backpack. With two, three, or four bricks weighing about 22 pounds (10 kg) each loaded onto his back, a worker would hike up the mountainside to the bricklayers waiting above.

Modern workers sometimes carry bricks for repairs on the Great Wall much like original workers would have done.

The wall sections between the towers were paved with tile. The wall and its towers were topped with ramparts and battlements made from bricks. These structures protected the soldiers who lived in the towers. The ramparts contained loopholes, or slits, for archers to shoot through and openings for cannons. The ramparts were functional, but they were also designed to be attractive. The walls nearest the capital were designed and installed with the utmost care for architectural refinement. The Ming wall boasts a great number of these watchtowers, far more than the original wall. General Qi Jiguang was governor of Jizhou province and one of the nine generals in charge of construction. He advised that watchtowers be built at every point the wall changed direction. This included high outcroppings and mountain peaks, every 109 yards (100 m) between points that were not as steep, and every 218 yards (200 m) along gentle slopes. Qi Jiguang oversaw the construction of thousands of watchtowers in the approximately 450 miles (720 km) between Beijing and Shanhaiguan. The region was never attacked by invaders as a result of the impenetrability of Qi Jiguang's section of the Great Wall.

The Ming Great Wall has the most architecturally advanced structures of the entire Great Wall. Gatehouses and fortresses were placed at intervals throughout the entire wall. These secure points were highly controlled and strongly defended. They were also built artistically. With its winged pagoda-style roofs brightly painted, the Jiayuguan fortress looks like a temple. The gatehouse structure is made from yellow brick inserted at different angles around the arches of the gates, which creates a mosaiclike effect.

Ming Innovations

In addition to design achievements, the Ming wall boasted a number of technological innovations that made it the pride of the empire. The Wanli emperor ordered the installation of a system of storm drains to lessen damage done to the wall by rainwater and snowmelt. These sewers drew off excess water from the wall without compromising its defenses—the water poured southward, toward China's interior. The Wanli emperor

Other Famous Walls

Other nations have famous walls. While they are not as physically notable as the Great Wall, they have their places in history and are known by people worldwide.

Romans once ruled the area that is present-day England and Wales. They feared attack by warriors to the north. To protect his people from invaders, Roman Emperor Hadrian (117–138 CE) built a wall across northern England that runs from the North Sea to the Irish Sea for nearly 75 miles (120 km). Today, the wall is known as Hadrian's Wall.

Following World War II (1939–1945 CE), Germany was divided into West Germany and East Germany. The city of Berlin was split into West Berlin and East Berlin. The United States, France, and the United Kingdom oversaw West Germany. The Soviet Union exerted control over East Germany. In 1961, the East Germans finished building an 858-mile (1380-km) line of fortification dividing Germany and Berlin. It included walls 12 to 15 feet (3.7 to 4.6 m) high, fences, machine-gun nests, attack dogs, and watchtowers. The barrier was built to keep East Germans from escaping to the West. The portion dividing Berlin was known as the Berlin Wall. Thousands of people tried to escape from East to West; more than 100 were killed. The Berlin Wall was torn down in 1990.

also proudly positioned replicas of Portuguese-made cannons along the tops of the watchtowers.

The Ming sections of the Great Wall were the pride of the empire. Completing the construction project required a tremendous amount of resources and cost many lives, although not as many as were said to have been sacrificed during the building of the Wall of Qin. The Ming wall segments, watchtowers, and garrison towers near Badaling, north of Beijing, are what most people think of when they visualize the Great Wall of China. These segments have inspired the imagination of citizens and visitors for centuries. Although the wall extended east and west in much the same way it had under Shi Huangdi, the section north of Beijing is the most spectacular feat of ancient engineering and human determination.

Reign Names

Chinese emperors chose a title, or name, for their reign. This name is intended to refer to the reign and is different from the emperor's personal name. For example, Cheng-zu selected Yongle as his reign title. Yongle is Chinese for "everlasting joy." When referring to this emperor, one would say Emperor Cheng-zu or the Yongle emperor.

The Wall's Decline

Focus on and care of the Great Wall declined after the Wanli emperor's great expansion, during his reign. The Wanli emperor's rule marked the

The Ming wall was the last great expansion of the Great Wall of China.

beginning of the end of the Ming dynasty. The emperor did not manage finances or China well. The Wanli emperor died in 1620 and was succeeded by three emperors who were also poor rulers. China continued to decline, and the Great Wall suffered. The emperors' lack of money meant that the wall could not be worked on—no expansions, no repairs. Lack of finances also meant that there was no way to pay for and provide supplies to the soldiers stationed at the wall. This lack of money resulted in the decline of the wall's upkeep.

Within a matter of a couple of decades, interest in the Great Wall had decreased drastically. It was simply no longer useful as a means of defense, so the Chinese government saw no need to maintain the wall as previous leaders had. To the Chinese, the wall was merely part of the landscape.

The Great Wall, with the Wanli emperor's perfections near Beijing, defended the Chinese empire of the Ming until 1644, when an army of Manchu fighters squeezed past the Great Wall where it ends in the Yellow Sea at Shanhaiguan, or Shanhai Pass. Ming Border General Wu Sangui opened the wall's gates at Shanhai Pass. Both sides—Ming and Manchu—considered Wu Sangui's actions treasonable. On May 26, Beijing fell to the Manchu army. The famed Ming dynasty was overthrown. A new dynasty emerged: the Qing dynasty. Emperors of the Qing dynasty would rule China for more than 250 years.

Leadership under the Qing emperors was very different than it had been during the reign of other dynasties. The Qing used religion and politics to control areas such as Mongolia to the north and Tibet to the south. As a result, the Qing emperors and subsequent rulers essentially ignored the wall

because it was no longer needed as
means for defending the country.

With the lack of interest in
maintaining the wall, it began to
vanish, falling victim to time and
the elements. This was especially so
in the west, where it had been made
of stamped earth, gravel, and twigs.
The wind and rain dissolved the wall.
In the east, soldiers had abandoned
their posts, so the daily care and attention the men
once provided to the wall ceased to exist. As a result,
a single crack left unfixed would expand and contract
from moisture freezing and thawing repeatedly with
the change of seasons. Over the course of several
years, a crack would grow until a brick would pop
out or a section would collapse. Throughout the
centuries, even the mighty granite and kiln-dried
bricks of the Wanli emperor's Ming wall cracked and
tumbled.

The last year that the Great Wall served any
military purpose was 1644. After the Qing overthrew
the Ming, the wall was ignored by the emperors, but
it would not be forgotten by future generations.

A crumbling section of the Great Wall near the rebuilt Jiayuguan Fort

Workers rebuild one of the few remaining sections of the Ming wall as part of an effort to preserve historical sites in Beijing, China.

The Wall Today

The Qing was China's last dynasty. The Republican Revolution (1911–1912 CE) brought China's long imperial history to an end. Henry Pu Yi was China's last emperor. He became emperor in 1908, when he was only two years old.

On February 12, 1912, Pu Yi was forced to abdicate, or give up, his throne. Following Pu Yi's stepping down in 1912, the Republic of China was formed. China was wrought with strife. First, there was a struggle between warlords during the Warlord Era (1916–1928 CE). Next, the nationalists and the communists fought in a full-scale civil war. The civil war was put on hold as the two sides formed the United Front during a brutal and bloody occupation by Japan in the 1930s and 1940s. The occupation ended when Allied forces defeated the Japanese in 1945 and World War II was brought to an end. But the end of the occupation did not end the turmoil in China. The country's civil war resumed in 1945. It ended with the declaration of the People's Republic of China, a communist regime, on October 1, 1949.

The Chinese communists had two very different opinions regarding China's past and the relics remaining from their nation's long history. One group sought to preserve China's rich cultural heritage. The other

Quebec City's Walls

Quebec City is the capital of the Canadian province of Quebec and the province's second-largest city. Established as a French fort in 1535 and founded as a city in 1608, it is one of the oldest cities in North America. The old quarter of Quebec City is North America's only walled city. Quebec's walls were built in the 1600s by the city's French population as protection from hostile Native Americans and the rival imperialists, the British. The seventeenth-century fortifications can still be seen today.

believed that ancient works of art and monuments such as the Great Wall served as painful reminders of the country's brutal past. This group felt that such relics should be destroyed. Chairman Mao Zedong, China's leader, was part of this group. Under his leadership, many parts of the wall and several Chinese relics were destroyed.

WELCOMING THE WORLD

Although Mao Zedong destroyed priceless Chinese artifacts, he made diplomatic advances. After more

---

"Confessions of the Great Wall"

Written in 1972, Huang Xiang's poem "Confessions of the Great Wall" is an example of the conflicts within China about the Chinese past and its monuments. The following is an excerpt from that poem:

I remind them
Of the subjugation and enclosure of
    countless generations past
Of the fear and hatred of ages
Of the struggles of those dark centuries,
    the sacrifices and suffering
Of the cacophonous divisions and
    disharmony
Of the furious history of human conflict
They want to overturn me, demolish me
For the sake of those ancestors of theirs
    who died within these mental walls
In order, for the first time, to leave to
    their sons and grandsons the legacy of
    science and democracy
. . .
Those places that were so distant in the
    past
Are now very near
My ramparts are disappearing from the
    earth's surface
Falling down within human minds
I am going   I have died
A generation of sons and grandsons are
    carrying me into the museum. . .[1]

than two decades of isolation, China began to open up to the rest of the world during the 1970s. The Great Wall served as an ambassador for China. It was a featured stop for U.S. President Richard Nixon during his historic visit in February 1972. This history-making visit to China by a U.S. president provided an opportunity to repair relations following decades of hostility.

Nixon Visits China

The day after Richard Nixon arrived in China in February 1972, he visited the Great Wall with Mao Zedong, China's leader. Nixon said of the wall, "This is a great wall and it had to be built by a great people."[3]

Late 1900s–Early 2000s

Mao Zedong died on September 9, 1976. He was succeeded by Deng Xiaoping, who favored preservation of China's cultural past. As a result, the Great Wall became a symbol of China—its construction was a monumental feat and a source of Chinese pride. After centuries of neglect, sections of the wall began to be repaired during the 1980s. Deng Xiaoping ushered in an era of restoration of the wall, saying in 1984, "Let us love our country and restore our Great Wall."[2] The wall was strengthened and polished. The Great Wall became a popular destination for Chinese and foreign visitors.

Children perform on the Great Wall in Beijing to celebrate the one-year countdown to the 2008 Olympic Games.

Restoration of the wall has continued into the new millennium. In July 2001, Beijing was named host of the 2008 Summer Olympics. China spent billions of dollars readying the Great Wall for the tourists who would visit the wall. Gansu province spent $9.7 million conserving the 124 miles (200 km) of Qin wall and 249 miles (400 km) of Han wall that still stand in the region. The Great Wall had once extended more than 1,243 miles (2,000 km) through Gansu alone, but most of it had crumbled and vanished over the centuries.

Renewed interest in the Great Wall during recent decades has led to preservation efforts, particularly lesser-visited sections in more remote provinces. However, not all sections of the Great Wall are being preserved. In contrast to conservation efforts in places such as Gansu province, many of the ancient walls surrounding Beijing have been demolished to make way for new roads, factories, and apartments. Still, as has been the case throughout much of the Great Wall's long history, the Chinese government is determined to repair and maintain it. Chinese national pride and wealth have contributed to the renewed determination to restore and care for the Great Wall.

The Great Wall has served a variety of roles throughout the centuries: defender and unifier of the Chinese people, guide to traders and travelers, and ambassador to the world. Its creation and rebuilding were

The Great Firewall of China

The spread of technology across the globe has introduced the Internet to many Chinese. However, this does not mean that computer-savvy Chinese can access all the information available on the Web. The Chinese government has established the Golden Shield Project, which is also known as the Great Firewall of China. As a result of the project, material deemed unacceptable by the government, including entire Web sites, cannot be accessed by people living in China. The project affects e-mail as well. Messages containing words such as democracy are discarded rather than sent to the intended recipient.

The Great Green Wall

During recent decades, China has been creating a new wall: the Great Green Wall. The project began in 1978. The goal is to plant a barrier of trees that will stop the erosion of the land and the expansion of the Gobi Desert. If successful, the Great Green Wall will block the sandstorms that strike Beijing every spring. The Chinese refer to these storms as the "yellow dragon."

The trees are being planted on approximately 2,800 miles (4,500 km) of land in northwest China along the Gobi Desert and follow the path of the Ming portion of the Great Wall. Since the beginning of the project, hundreds of millions of trees have been planted. They are mostly Chinese elms. The building of the Great Green Wall is expected to last until at least 2050. In addition to planting a new forest, the Chinese government is promoting conservation of China's current forests.

backbreaking and heartbreaking, but the Chinese have come to look upon the wall in a favorable light. Today, the wall connects them with a shared pride. The Great Wall also unites the world, attracting travelers from the global community who gather in awe and appreciation of the monument and the culture and history it represents. The mighty structure that winds like a snake through China's varied terrain is much more than a wall. The Great Wall of China is a fitting tribute to China's long and varied history and the durability and splendor of Chinese civilization.

The Great Wall is a fitting tribute to China's history and
to Chinese civilization.

TIMELINE

5000 BCE	circa 2100s–1600s BCE	circa 1650–1027 BCE
Ancient people settle along China's rivers in farming villages and build walls for protection.	The Xia dynasty rules China.	The Shang dynasty rules China.

221–214 BCE	206 BCE–220 CE	317–589 CE
The Wall of Qin is constructed.	Emperors of the Han dynasty rule China. The Great Wall experiences its first major expansion.	China is divided into the Northern and Southern dynasties.

circa 1027–221 BCE

The Zhou dynasty rules China.

circa 475–221 BCE

The many regions of China fight during the Warring States period.

221 BCE

Shi Huangdi becomes the first emperor of China, and the Qin dynasty begins.

589 CE

China is reunified under the Sui dynasty (581–618 CE).

618–907 CE

China becomes a world power during the Tang dynasty, and art and culture flourish.

907–960 CE

China is divided a second time into northern and southern regions.

TIMELINE

960–1279 CE	1215 CE	1279–1368 CE
Emperors of the Song dynasty reunify and rule China. The Chinese make great strides in science and technology.	Genghis Khan becomes ruler of China north of the Huai River, beginning an era of Mongol rule.	Mongol emperors of the Yuan dynasty rule all of China.

1930s and 1940s CE	1949 CE	1972 CE
Japan occupies China.	China becomes the People's Republic of China.	In February, Richard Nixon becomes the first U.S. president to visit China and the Great Wall.

1368–1644 CE	1644–1911 CE	1912 CE
Emperors of the Ming dynasty rule China and make the last great expansion to the Great Wall.	Emperors of the Manchu, or Qing, dynasty rule China. They are China's last emperors.	The last emperor steps down on February 12, and the Republic of China is formed.

1980s CE	2001 CE	2008 CE
Deng Xiaoping ushers in renewed interest in preserving the Great Wall.	China is named host of the 2008 Summer Olympics and begins restoring the Great Wall in preparation of the event.	China hosts the Summer Olympics in August.

Essential Facts

Purpose

The Great Wall of China began as the Wall of Qin. It was constructed to defend China's northern border from barbarian neighbors in northern lands. Shi Huangdi also built his wall, which became the Great Wall, to unify his country. Citizens who were once separated by village and regional boundaries were unified by the wall. Once members of warring tribes, millions of Chinese were brought together under a single ruler and forced to work on his project. The wall also kept foreigners out, isolating the Chinese from other peoples and cultures.

Dimensions

❖ Length estimates: 2,400 miles (3,862 km) to 3,930 miles (6,325 km)

❖ Average height: 20–30 feet (6–9 m)

❖ Average width: 25 feet (8 m) at the base, tapering to 15 feet (5 m) at the top

Primary Phases of Construction

❖ The Qin dynasty completes the first Great Wall, the Wall of Qin, in 214 BCE.

❖ The Han dynasty (206 BCE–220 CE) extends the Wall of Qin. Wu Di orders a 300-mile (483-km) extension, including "a beacon every 5 li, a tower every 10 li, a fort every 30 li, and a castle every 100 li."

❖ The Ming dynasty (1368–1644 CE) oversees the last major expansion of the wall with notable changes under the Yongle emperor (1403–1424 CE), the Chenghua emperor (1464–1487 CE), and the Wanli emperor (1572–1620 CE).

BUILDING MATERIALS

❖ The materials used to build the Great Wall varied by region and with time.

❖ The Wall of Qin was constructed of earth, stones, and wood. Desert sections included twigs.

❖ Later additions and reconstructions were built with granite, bricks, tiles, and lime.

DESIGN

The Great Wall consists of thousands of garrison towers and watchtowers joined by sections of wall. The massive brick-and-stone garrison towers were erected every few miles to house guards. The watchtowers were spaced every few hundred yards and were approximately 39 feet (12 m) high. The base was 39 feet (12 m) across and narrowed toward the top to approximately 30 feet (9 m). The sections of wall built to join the towers were approximately 24 feet (7 m) tall and wide enough for eight men to march abreast in formation. The Ming expansion included increasing the heights of towers and making them suitable for using cannons. In addition, the towers were designed to be places for storage and to house the soldiers who were stationed at them.

COST

Construction of the Wall of Qin was expensive in terms of actual cost. Building the wall was also costly to the Chinese in nonmonetary ways. Hundreds of thousands of men from across the country were forced into laboring on the project, including farmers and their workers. Many laborers died in the building of the wall. In addition, the lack of workers available to farm the land resulted in a food shortage across the vast empire.

ADDITIONAL RESOURCES

SELECT BIBLIOGRAPHY

Fairbank, John King, and Merle Goldman. *China: A New History*. Cambridge, MA: Harvard University Press, 2006.

Fryer, Jonathan. *The Great Wall of China*. New York: A.S. Barnes & Co, 1977.

Silverberg, Robert. *The Great Wall of China*. New York: Chilton Books, 1965.

Waldron, Arthur. *The Great Wall of China: From History to Myth*. Cambridge, Eng.: Cambridge University Press, 1990.

FURTHER READING

Cheng, Dalin. *The Great Wall of China*. Hong Kong, PRC: South China Morning Post Ltd/New China News Ltd., 1984.

Green, Robert. *China: Modern Nations of the World*. San Diego, CA: Lucent Books, 1999.

Lindesay, Charles. *The Great Wall (Genius of China Close-up Guide)*. Hong Kong, PRC: Odyssey Publications, 1998.

Zewen, Luo, Dai Wenbao, Dick Wilson, Jean-Pierre Drege, and Hubert DeLahaye. *The Great Wall*. London: Michael Joseph Ltd., 1981.

Web Links

To learn more about the Great Wall of China, visit ABDO
Publishing Company online at **www.abdopublishing.com**.
Web sites about the Great Wall of China are featured on our Book
Links page. These links are routinely monitored and updated to
provide the most current information available.

Places to Visit

Badaling
Beijing, China
www.greatwallbeijing.com
Conveniently located approximately 43 miles (70 km) northwest of
Beijing, Badaling is the best preserved and most visited section of
the Great Wall.

The Forbidden City
Beijing, China
www.forbiddencitychina.com
Built by the Ming in the 1400s as home to the emperor, the
Forbidden City is located in the center of Beijing. The city includes
800 buildings and is open every day of the year.

**Museum of the Terra-Cotta Warriors and Horses of Qin
Shihuang (Qin Shi Huangdi)**
Lintong County, Shaanxi Province
+86-029-81399170
www.bmy.com.cn
Thousands of terra-cotta figures from the first Qin emperor's
tomb are on display, including warriors, horses, and chariots.
Tours in English are available.

GLOSSARY

barbarian
People considered inferior. In Chinese history, these were often the tribes living north of China.

bastion
A stronghold. A defensive position that is strengthened or well fortified.

battlement
A parapet around a defensive structure, such as a wall or a watchtower, with cutouts through which arrows, guns, or cannons are shot.

dynasty
A group of rulers who belong to the same family for multiple generations. Commonly, a succession of grandfathers, fathers, sons, grandsons, and so on.

emperor
The head male monarch of an empire.

garrison tower
A structure placed every few miles along the Great Wall in which troops could sleep and eat.

hangtu
Chinese for "tamped earth," a method of building walls in which earth is packed in layers.

jade
A green colored semi-precious stone that was frequently carved into ornamental pieces in the Far East.

khan
Title for the military and political leader among the Mongols (Tartars) and other Central Asian nomadic peoples.

li
A Chinese mile, it is equivalent to .3 miles (.5 km).

mausoleum
A large tomb that is often a building made of stone. Rather than burying the dead, the bodies are placed above ground in the building.

mortar
A compound of sand, lime, or cement and water that is used to bind bricks together.

nomads
People who travel from place to place instead of settling down in a location. Nomads are usually herders.

outcroppings
The portions of rock formations that come out of the ground.

parapet
A short wall above the edge of a defensive wall that protects the guards on top from enemy arrows.

rampart
A defensive wall topped with a parapet or battlement.

Silk Road
A series of roads through western China and Central Asia by which caravans transporting trade goods, especially silk, reached the Middle East and Europe.

steppes
A dry, treeless, grassy area.

terra-cotta
A fired clay used to create statues, vessels, and building materials, such as tiles and ornaments.

SOURCE NOTES

Chapter 1. Land of Achievements
1. Mildred Cable and Francesca French. *The Gobi Desert*. London: Hodder & Stoughton, 1946. 13–14.
2. "About World Heritage." *Unesco.org*. 2008. 24 June 2008 <http://whc.unesco.org/en/about/>.

Chapter 2. Ancient China

1. Julia Lovell. *The Great Wall: China Against the World: 1000 BC–AD 2000*. New York: Grove Press, 2006. 34.
2. Ontario Consultants on Religious Tolerance. "Taoism." *Religioustolerance.org*. 2008. 24 June 2008 <http://www.religioustolerance.org/taoism.htm>.

Chapter 3. Imperial and Modern China
None

Chapter 4. Unifying a Nation
1. James Legge, Trans. *The Chinese Classics: The She King*. Taipei, Tw.: Wen-shih-che, 1971. 263.
2. Owen Lattimore. *Studies in Frontier History: Collected Papers 1929–1958*. London: Oxford University Press, 1962. 116.

Chapter 5. Building the Wall of Qin
1. Julia Lovell. *The Great Wall: China Against the World: 1000 BC–AD 2000*. New York: Grove Press, 2006. 60.

Chapter 6. The Wall after Qin: 206 BCE–1368 CE
1. "Great Wall of China." *Encyclopædia Britannica*. 2008. Encyclopædia Britannica Online. 25 June 2008 <http://www.britannica.com/eb/article-92933>.
2. Julia Lovell. *The Great Wall: China Against the World: 1000 BC–AD 2000*. New York: Atlantic Books, 2006. 110.

Chapter 7. The Ming Dynasty
1. William Edgar Geil. *The Great Wall of China*. New York: Sturgis & Walton Co. 1909. 98–99.

Chapter 8. A Final Great Expansion
1. Julia Lovell. *The Great Wall: China Against the World: 1000 BC–AD 2000*. New York: Atlantic Books, 2006. 257.

Chapter 9. The Wall Today
1. Julia Lovell. *The Great Wall: China Against the World: 1000 BC–AD 2000*. New York: Atlantic Books, 2006. 324–326.
2. "The Great Wall of China: Tangible, Intangible and Destructible." *China Heritage Newsletter*. Mar. 2005. China Heritage Project. 2007. Research School of Pacific and Asian Studies (RSPAS), Australian National University. 26 June 2008 <http://www.chinaheritagenewsletter.org/features.php?searchterm=001_greatwall.inc&issue=001>.
3. Julia Lovell. *The Great Wall: China Against the World: 1000 BC–AD 2000*. New York: Atlantic Books, 2006. 323.

INDEX

INDEX CONTINUED

ABOUT THE AUTHOR

Joseph R. O'Neill is a historian, an author, and a freelance journalist. He has a bachelor's degree in classics and history from Monmouth College and a master's degree in ancient history from the University of Illinois. O'Neill has written several books and articles on a variety of historical and literary topics and was a contributing author for the *Encyclopedia of the Ancient Greek World* (2006). He lives in Los Angeles, California.

PHOTO CREDITS

Dallas and John Heaton/Free Agents Limited/Corbis, cover; Jin shizi/Imaginechina/AP Images, 6; Bridgeman-Giraudon/Art Resource, NY, 8, 38; Red Line Editorial, 10, 16, 25, 33, 47, 58, 84; Greg Baker/AP Images, 15, 44, 87, 88; North Wind Picture Archives, 19; AP Images, 23; Dick Druckman/AP Images, 26; Bildarchiv Preussischer Kulturbesitz/Art Resource, NY, 30; HIP/Art Resource, NY, 34; Chien-Min Chung/AP Images, 37; Mark Avery/AP Images, 43; Adrian Bradshaw/epa/Corbis, 53; Redlink/Corbis, 54, 80; National Palace Museum/AP Images, 65; Wolfgang Kaehler/Corbis, 66; Vincent Yu/AP Images, 68; James Sparshatt/Corbis, 72; Steven Vidler/Eurasia Press/Corbis, 75; So Hing-Keung/Corbis, 76; Zhang qingyun/ Imaginechina/AP Images, 92; Steve Allen/Jupiterimages/AP Images, 95